W9-DET-856

The $52.⁰⁰ Seed Miracle

52 Testimonials Revealing God's Uncommon, Supernatural, Divine Favor

Bishop E. Bernard Jordan

FOGHORN
PUBLISHERS

All Scripture quotations, unless otherwise indicated, are taken from the Holy Bible, New International Version® NIV® Copyright 1973, 1978, 1984 by International Bible Society, The King James Version, and the Amplified Version. Used by permission.

The $52.00 Seed Miracle: 52 Testimonies Revealing God's Uncommon, Supernatural, Divine Favor

Zoe Ministries
310 Riverside Drive
New York, NY 10025
(212) 316-2177
(212) 316-5769 (fax)

ISBN-10: 1-934466-05-0
ISBN-13: 978-1-934466-05-6
Printed in the United States of America
©2008 by E. Bernard Jordan. All Rights Reserved.

Foghorn Publishers
P.O. Box 8286
Manchester, CT 06040-0286
860-216-5622
860-290-8291 fax.
foghornpublisher@aol.com

No part of this book may be reproduced or transmitted in any form or by any means, electronic or mechanical, including photocopying, recording, or by any information storage and retrieval system, without permission in writing from the publisher.

Prophetic Partners

I would like to thank each of these prophetic partners for sowing a seed toward this book. Their financial seeds have made it possible for you to be able to receive this book without charge to you. May God add life to every giver, for through your gift you are causing life to perpetuate in others.

Bishop AJ Collins

Lady Shebra Collins

Tania Thornton

Angela M. Carter

Mascareen Cohen

Alice Jackson

Loreen Floris

Anthony Reid

Bernadette Joseph

Julia Fortune

Sheffian Joseph

Jacqueline Jefferies

Antoinette John

Ikhisha Levell

Denise Josephs Stewart

Cheron and Clarence Moran

Roberta Freeman

The Guy Family

Barbara Tucker Fugate

Margaret Sweney

Melissa Johnson

Demsey Rodney

A CALL TO ACTION!

"If ye have faith as a grain of mustard seed, ye shall say unto this mountain, Remove hence to yonder place; and it shall remove; and nothing shall be impossible unto you."
(Matthew 17:20)

As you begin to read this amazing compilation of testimonies, I have two questions for you—Are you ready for a miracle? AND Are you ready for UNCOMMON, SUPERNATURAL, UNMERITED, INSURMOUNTABLE, HUMONGOUS, LONG OVERDUE FAVOR? Well, can I tell you that you are next in line for the fullness of God to manifest in your life?

You have been asking God for a miracle. You have been asking God to change your current situation. You have witnessed others around you being blessed daily, while you sit on the sidelines saying, "God, when is it my turn?" Well, I have good news for you. The Bible says that God is no respecter of persons. But you have to trust God. Although it may appear that others are moving ahead of you, God says, "Your best is yet to come!" Although it may appear that others are advancing in their careers, relationships and finances, God says, "Your latter days will be greater than your formers days." Although it looks like you are always dwelling in the "land of not enough," God says, "If you decree a thing, it shall come to pass."

On Friday night, November 30, 2007, during our Power of Prophecy Live Steaming Telecast, while in the process of prophesying to many of my partners, I sensed the anguish, disappointment, grief and despair that were taking place in the lives of some of my partners, their friends and family members. Instantly, God spoke to me and said, "I want to release 52 weeks of uncommon favor in the lives of those who have the courage to believe the prophet." I further heard God say, "Challenge the people to sow a $52.00 seed, and by their faith I will release 52 weeks of uncommon favor in their lives."

Once I released this decree to sow the seed of $52.00 for 52 weeks of uncommon favor, the atmosphere changed and God began opening the door to His Divine Favor. The streaming audience began to feel the vibration. The phones started ringing off the hook. The atmosphere was charged with the power of God. My partners from all over the world were calling in their $52.00 seeds for themselves, their family members and their friends. Then the atmosphere shifted again and our faith was pushed to another level. One of my partners called in and decided to sow $5,200 for 52 weeks of uncommon favor! Not only that, others began calling in their $520.00 seeds for uncommon favor! People began to stretch their faith and take God at His word.

From that day forward, the $52.00 seed miracle has been working wonders. We have received hundreds of powerful testimonies proclaiming the miraculous victories people are experiencing as a result of sowing the seed and working their faith. As I began to share the testimonies with my streaming audience in the weeks following God's powerful decree, people were being blessed and their faith was increasing daily. We are truly overcome by the word of our testimony.

I am believing God for 52,000 people to share their testimonies of how the $52.00 seed (or gradations of the same) has opened their lives to UNCOMMON, INSURMOUNTABLE, ALL-ENCOMPASSING, DIVINE FAVOR! We are in a season where God wants to demonstrate His power in the earth in miraculous ways. God wants to shine His glory through the lives of people and let the world know that He is Lord.

God does not waste His words. He never says something for the sake of being heard. When He speaks, He means what He says. There is a major struggle going on in the lives of believers all over the world, and many are not equipped to fight the battles that are before them. But when God decides to release His anointing, it is for the betterment of all who are in tune with His Spirit. God has made a promise to us that He is releasing 52 weeks of uncommon favor that will equip the believer to fight "the good fight of faith." During this dispensation, God is going to use YOUR life and YOUR testimony to heal the land.

I feel deliverance taking place. I feel the abundance of financial increase taking place. I feel healing taking place. The same power and anointing that was with us on that powerful Friday night, is still with us today. After reading so many testimonies about the 52 weeks of uncommon favor, I am not only motivated, but I am persuaded that God is up to something bigger than we can ever imagine.

Won't you be one of the 52,000 believers who have decided to share their testimony with the world about the miracle of the $52.00 seed? Won't you be one of the 52,000 believers who dared to believe God and who have the courage to come back to Him to say, "Thank You." I encourage you to put your faith to the test and join us on this powerful journey of 52 weeks of uncommon favor. I can guarantee, your life will never be the same!

Master Prophet E. Bernard Jordan

P.S. Don't leave out your family members and friends. Sow a $52.00 seed on their behalf and allow them to experience the favor of God with you.

Remember, your money won't be late in 2008!

UNCOMMON FAVOR!

"And they overcame him by the blood of the Lamb,
and by the word of their testimony…"
(Revelation 12:11)

In November 2007, God spoke to me concerning the $52.00 seed and challenged His people to sow and position themselves to receive 52 weeks of uncommon favor. When God spoke to me about the 52 weeks of favor, I had no idea of the impact it would have on the people of God. But from that day forward, God has been opening doors of opportunity and releasing favor unto those who hearken unto His voice and obey His command.

The hand of God has been so evident over the last few months, that the Holy Spirit told me to pen a work detailing 52 powerful testimonies of people who dared to believe God and walk into His Divine Favor. The testimonies are still pouring in everyday about the miracles that God is doing in the lives of believers all over the world. God's promise of 52 weeks of uncommon favor was so powerful that it caused one my partners to sow multiple $5,200 seeds, others to sow the seed of $520.00, and so many others to sow the seed of $52.00. The power of God has been so amazing that people are now sowing multiple $52.00 seeds for themselves, for their family members and for their friends. God is truly doing something great in the lives of His people!

TESTIMONY #1

"After I sowed my second $52.00 seed, I applied for an alternative educational loan. In the past, I had applied three times for a student loan, but I was always denied. The day after I sowed the $52.00 seed for 52 weeks of favor, I was approved. I am now able to continue my educational endeavors. Praise God!"
(K.C., New Jersey)

Did you know that God has 52 weeks of uncommon favor in store for you? As I pen the words of this powerful testimonial, I can literally feel the pains of transition that you have been going through. You have been dealing with some of the most difficult situations that you have ever encountered. But I hear the word of the Lord saying, "The worst is over and the best is yet to come!"

DIVINE FAVOR!

"God Almighty bless thee, and make thee fruitful... and give thee the blessing of Abraham, that thou mayest inherit the land wherein thou art a stranger, which God gave unto Abraham."
(Genesis 28:3-4)

Since God has declared the 52 weeks of uncommon favor, I have been inundated with biblical revelation in the Scriptures where the sequence of the numbers 5 and 2 appear. According to the book of Genesis, when Jacob journeyed toward the land of Haran to work for his uncle, he seemed to have many strikes against him. He had been forced to leave home; his brother had threatened to kill him; he was moving toward 52 years of age; and he had nothing of tangible value to help him succeed. However, although his assets were intangible, Jacob had everything necessary for success. As he prepared to make his journey, his father gave him a blessing appropriate for a future millionaire.

After you plan for your success, there are several definite success principles necessary to help your master plan come true. The $52.00 seed for uncommon favor will position you for a year of results.

> *"Are not five sparrows sold for two farthings,*
> *and not one of them is forgotten before God?"*
> *(Luke 12:6)*

In Luke 12:6, Jesus reminds us of our intrinsic worth. Your daily struggles may cause you to feel as if God has forgotten about you, but like the sparrow, you are always on the mind of God. He is preparing you for a financial miracle that is going shock the people around you.

Favor Principle #1

There is a <u>5</u> and a <u>2</u> working together to get you the blessings that you deserve!

TESTIMONY #2

"As a result of sowing the $52.00 seed, God has truly blessed me and my family! I am a single parent of four children. I had to trust God to bless my children this holiday, and He has blessed me to go on four holiday shopping sprees. I was even able to bless other families out of my abundance. Money even showed up at my door from an anonymous giver! The blessings of the Lord make us rich and add no sorrow. Thank you, Bishop Jordan for the word of the Lord."
(J.W., Virginia Beach, VA)

The Holy Spirit is working overtime in your life to reveal to you just how important you are in the eyes of God. I hear God saying, "Your net worth is growing steadily and will increase over the next 52 weeks." God wants to restore to you everything that has been snatched from you over the last 5 years and 2 weeks.

Favor Principle #2

Nature abhors a vacuum.

Nature abhors a vacuum. When you empty yourself, the universe will fill you with much more. Voluntary giving is an acknowledgement to God that you understand and accept His system. You must always give up something in order to gain something. Generally, it is whatever blocks you from depending solely on God. In this equation of personal and universal economy, like attracts like. You must understand and live by this principle, if you are going to reap the harvest and live in harmony with God's economic system.

TESTIMONY #3

"I sowed the $52.00 seed for 52 weeks of favor, and favor has been coming my way. On December 17, 2007, I contacted Toys for Tots online to request toy donations for children who attend my day care facility, whose parents were unable to purchase Christmas gifts for them. The Toys for Tots website stipulated that an organization had to be classified as a 501(c)(3) entity to benefit from their program, of which my program does not have that classification. However, I checked the list of sponsors and contacted two of them.

One of the sponsors returned my call, and on Saturday, December 23, 2007, I was informed to bring garbage bags to their offices and pick up the toys. They told me to give the toys to the families in need and to keep some for my day care, as well!. I left there with 10 bags of toys! Praise God! Thank you, Master Prophet for giving me the opportunity to believe God and walk into divine favor." **(S.W., Newark, DE)**

TESTIMONY #4

"I sowed the $52.00 seed for 52 weeks of favor, and the blessings are overflowing in my life. I even saw my friend receive a blessing as a result of the first $52.00 seed that I sowed. I am being blessed in every area of my life. Favor is overtaking my life. Thank you, Master Prophet for helping me!" **(T.G., Norristown, PA)**

You have been anointed and appointed by God to be a conduit of wealth. God wants to put millions in your hands. You may be wondering, "How can I be a provider when I don't have millions right now?" Your ability to be a provider has nothing to do with what you have in the physical realm. It has everything to do with the way you think and your willingness to simply obey the voice of God.

TESTIMONY #5

"What can I say, favor just keeps on coming!!! First of all, I am talking canceled debt and job recognition! I started working on my credit some months ago and it seemed like I was getting nowhere. But since sowing the $52.00 seed for 52 weeks of favor, I have had two debt cancellations and more to come! Not only that, I have finally received the recognition I deserve from my new boss, who continually disregarded my suggestions, saying, "That's not going to work; we're going to try something else." He would recognize everyone else's work, but my work was never recognized, until I sowed the $52.00 seed. Now, I can't get him to stop saying "Good job; keep up the good work!" He even asks for my opinion and help on special projects. Now, that's uncommon favor!" **(J.H., Duluth, GA)**

UNMERITED FAVOR!

"But he said unto them, I have meat
to eat that ye know not of."
(John 4:32)

According to Joel Goldsmith, once we come into God-consciousness, we are no longer under the law of supply and demand. You must learn to free yourself from the law of supply and demand. God throws us into dilemmas so that we can place a demand upon His anointing. When demand is put into place, then supply is of use. That is what faith is all about, doing the impossible, which opens the door to abundance.

What you hold on to, you lose; but what you release, you keep. Hoarding all that you have and saving what you believe to be your only supply can be a thing of the past, if only you will trust and believe the prophet.

Favor Principle #3

You are the sum total of your thoughts.

I hear the word of the Lord saying...

"This is your year to walk in the consciousness of no lack. Lack no longer has a place in your life. God wants to infuse your consciousness with the thoughts of prosperity."

TESTIMONY #6

"My sister sowed the $52.00 seed for me for 52 weeks of favor, because I did not have the money at the time to sow the seed, and I tell you, the favor has already started. A week after she sowed the seed, my husband gave me $300.00 to buy Christmas gifts. But

instead of buying gifts, I decided to take the money and open a checking and savings account and start my online business. To God be the glory for the 52 weeks of favor! Thank you, Master Prophet!" **(S.S., Foley, AL)**

LOOK AWAY FROM SHORTAGE
AND SEE INFINITE SUPPLY!

LONG, OVERDUE FAVOR!

"Come unto me all ye that labor and are heavy laden and I will give you rest. Take my yoke upon you and learn from me, for I am meek and lowly in heart and ye shall find rest for your souls."
(Matthew 11:28-29)

Long, overdue favor is on its way to you, but God wants you to rest in this season. Rest is given to those that go to God. When you go to God, God comes to you. God meets Himself in you. Our prayers are spoken in faith, and then released to the power of the law. Be still and know that God is working behind the scenes on your behalf.

TESTIMONY #7

"I sowed the $52.00 seed for 52 weeks of favor, and subsequently, I have experienced favor in my family relationships, particularly with my sister and brother-in-law. For years we have had difficulty communicating. But after sowing the $52.00 seed, I visited their home and we were able to have a very pleasant visit. They even showed support for my business ventures and gave me money and tools to help with the business. I know this is a result of the $52.00 seed of uncommon favor that I sowed. Thank you, Master Prophet."
(J.D., Denmark)

The Bible says that we are to think on those things that are lovely. Think on those things that are true. Think on those things that are honest. Think on those things that are pure. (Philippians 4:8) You have to be mindful of your thoughts. God wants you to think on those things that will bring peace, because peace is the state at which we create. Isaiah 26:3 says, "Thou wilt keep him in perfect peace, whose mind is stayed on thee: because he trusteth in thee." The mind has to be steadied in peace.

Favor Principle #4

Everything starts with your thoughts.

As a result of the $52.00 seed, relationships are being restored unto God's people; job promotions are manifesting in the lives of God's people; financial increase is overtaking God's people; and the list just keeps on growing! The Holy Spirit revealed to me that God is not going to let the 52 weeks of uncommon favor return back to Him void, but it will accomplish all that it has been destined to accomplish.

TESTIMONY #8

"I sowed the $52.00 seed for 52 weeks of uncommon favor and God is working miracles in my finances. I received uncommon favor concerning my medical expenses. Initially, I was paying close to $500.00 a month for my medical expenses. But after sowing the seed, I am only paying $150.00 a month. Thank God for His Divine Favor!" **(A.M., Salisbury, MD)**

TESTIMONY #9

"I sowed the $52.00 seed for 52 weeks of uncommon favor. Bishop Jordan, you have been prophesying favor in my relationships with family and friends, as well as favor over my finances. You said that I would have the best Christmas ever this year. Well, it happened! The Lord has blessed me and my family. The conversation in my house has changed for the good. On December 18th, we were able to celebrate my grandmother's 70th birthday. We almost lost her three times, but praise God for His favor!

I have been transformed by your ministry. I want to say thank you for listening and obeying the Holy Spirit regarding the 52 weeks of uncommon favor. As a result of my own obedience to the Holy

Spirit, I am now selling beauty supply products over the internet, and I am learning to generate multiple streams of income. Thank you, Master Prophet! I look forward to continuing my relationship with you." (**A.M., Madison, IL**)

INSURMOUNTABLE FAVOR!

"And all these blessings shall come on thee, and overtake thee, if thou shalt hearken unto the voice of the LORD thy God."
(Deuteronomy 28:2)

The favor of God is an awesome benefit that is available to everyone. Yet sadly, it is a power that too many of us live without. It is important to note that the favor of God does not mean that you will not experience events in your life that seem to be unfair. But favor steps in and corrects the errors in your life and works everything together for your good. When it appears that you are at a disadvantage, God steps in and gives you the advantage. When you are on the brink of defeat and failure, God will make you victorious in the end.

Fear not! God is in the process of opening doors in your life that were off limits to you in the past. Some of your closest friends have been trying to keep you in lack, but the Holy Spirit is recommending that you get a promotion in this season, courtesy of God. That is good news! You are in the midst of a season where you will find it virtually impossible to fail. God has already given you everything that you need to manifest the promise He has made to you.

TESTIMONY #10

"I sowed the $52.00 seed for the 52 weeks of uncommon favor and God is working miracles in my life. I was able to escape from a major automobile accident, which should have left me dead, unharmed! All I could do was call on the name of Jesus. Thank God for the 52 weeks of Divine Favor!

Also, the very thing that I have been believing God for, showed up at my door just like God told me it would. God is really blowing my mind! All I know is that you can't beat God giving! Thank you, Master Prophet, for your obedience to the voice of God and seeing into the Spirit what thus saith the Lord! My life will never be the same!" (**C.P., Sanford, FL**)

Favor Principle #5

Faith expands beyond the boundaries of reason.

UNMERITED FAVOR!

"Now faith is the substance of things hoped for,
the evidence of things not seen."
(Hebrews 11:1)

Faith totally contradicts reason. You cannot live within the realm of reason and expect your faith to work. You have to move beyond reason. You have to stretch and believe what you cannot see with your natural eye, so that you can experience success. God's favor equals success! If you are like me, you need supernatural favor working in your life all of the time!

TESTIMONY #11

"After sowing the $52.00 seed for 52 weeks of favor, God has been working in my relationships and in my finances. My relationship with my son is being restored; new and exciting ideas for my business are flooding my mind; and I was finally courageous enough to go into the studio to put some music to a project that I have been working on for the past year. People are even sharing their testimonies with me about how my music project is blessing their lives in a very powerful way. I now see infinite possibilities and prosperity in my life, and I am able to share and bless others by showing them how to do the same! Thank you, Master Prophet, for the opportunity to sow the seed!" **(D.S., Queens, NY)**

The purpose of faith is to encourage us to look beyond what our natural eye can see. God is always pushing us to move in our divinity. If you are going to walk in the supernatural, you must have faith. You must believe. If you believe and know that God only wants good for you, you will win in this season.

TESTIMONY #12

"Just another praise report about how God's favor is working on my behalf. I sowed the $52.00 seed for 52 weeks of uncommon favor. I owed my scholarship sponsor $52.00. After sowing the seed, my scholarship sponsor informed me that they owed me $192.00. They deducted the $52.00 that I owed to them and sent me a check for $140.00! Praise God for Favor!" **(S.W., Newark, DE)**

Favor Principle #6

Faith contradicts reason.

SUPERNATURAL FAVOR!

"Now I say, that the heir, as long as he is a child, differeth nothing from a servant, though he be lord of all."
(Galatians 4:1)

Your future is created from seed that the Father has placed in your hand. Your harvest is created from seed that the Father has placed in your hand. When you fail to work with what is in your hand you are not operating at your fullest potential. You are operating from a state of lack and limitation. It is time for you to shake yourself and get out of the place of lack. You are lord of all.

Jesus didn't come to reveal Himself; Jesus came to reveal who you are. Greatness lives in you! Divine Favor lives in you! The only Jesus you will ever meet is you!

TESTIMONY #13

"I sowed the $52.00 seed for 52 weeks of favor. You said that God would cause people to pay me back money that they owed me and that money would start coming to me. Well, it is happening! I am looking for the Lord to continue to do wonderful and mighty things in my life. I am looking for Him to bless me with my own place to stay and the ability to pay my rent in advance. Thank you, Master Prophet for your words of encouragement and your prayers. I appreciate you for standing in the gap on my behalf. I love you and praise God for you being a part of my life. Because of your teachings, I am learning what really is on the inside of me—the very essence of God!" **(E.P., Minneapolis, MN)**

TESTIMONY #14

"On December 18, 2007, I sowed the $52.00 seed for 52 weeks of favor. I named the seed, "No more debt! All bills are paid," believing

that all lack was being removed from my life. The Master Prophet prophesied that in 77 hours all sowers would see miracles. On Thursday, I was experiencing pain in my back, which I thought was gas. It moved into my chest area, but I am an extremely health-conscious person, so I didn't give it much thought. Friday, the pain continued and I thought it may be asthma. I tried to call my doctor and couldn't get through and decided to go to the emergency room. Much to my surprise, I was diagnosed with angina pectoris, a condition that precedes a heart attack. I am truly favored and blessed to be here! Thank you, Master Prophet, for the knowledge you sow within me!" **(R.G., Washington, D.C.)**

The only sight there is, is the gift of second sight; the realm where you are seeing from the Spirit, not with the natural eye. The natural eye is not our reality. There is a world more real behind your eyes than the world that is before your eyes. In which world do you believe? Do you believe in the world that is behind your eyes? Everything outside of you is a lie. You must live in the world that is behind your eyes.

Favor Principle #7

**You only become what you are
conscious of being.**

MAGNANIMOUS FAVOR!

"Blessed are the people of whom this is true;
blessed are the people whose God is the LORD."
(Psalm 144:15)

Favor is not something that you earn. It isn't something that you deserve. Favor is something that God freely gives to you. You cannot earn it; it is given to you! Don't try to figure it out, don't try to reason with it, and don't try to understand it; just flow with God and receive everything that God intends for you to have.

Favor Principle #8

God takes pleasure in the prosperity of his servants.

You must take a leap of faith and rid yourself of dependency and thoughts of lack and limitation before God can begin to work in your life. God wants you to relinquish your natural means of support and rely solely on Him. You have to clean out everything that is inside of you that negates Spirit and make room for what you truly desire. This season of 52 weeks of uncommon favor is the perfect season to empty yourself so that you may be filled with independence, realization of unlimited resources, and thoughts of abundance. Let God be your unlimited supply.

TESTIMONY #15

"I sowed the $52.00 seed for 52 weeks of uncommon favor, and favor has been overflowing in my life ever since. Since I sowed the seed, every store that I go into I am greeted as "Sir" and the salespeople help me to save money and get more for my dollar.

My family is coming back together and we are learning to work out our differences. I am now receiving my Worker's Compensation checks on time, and the doctor assigned to my case assured me that he would inform the adjuster that my injuries are legitimate.

The bill collectors, who were at one time denying me grace periods to pay off my bills, are now giving me more than enough time to pay them off. My job, that never gave anything, gave me a $50.00 dollar gift certificate. The local union I belong to gave me a $20.00 gift certificate for Christmas. My online college sent me a check for $1,557.52. Favor! Favor! Favor! Thank you, Bishop Jordan, for hearing from God and allowing me to be a part of this season of uncommon favor." **(A.D., Grand Rapids, MI)**

Everything has a vibration. You cannot come into the company of the rich until you have rich thoughts. You have to get into the atmosphere of celebration. What you celebrate will vibrate at your frequency.

TESTIMONY #16

"Master Prophet, thank you for the opportunity to sow the $52.00 seed for 52 weeks of favor. The Lord has sent you in my life, and I know that there is truth in your mouth. Because of your prophetic word to me, I no longer live in Brooklyn. Hallelujah! The house in Schenectady will soon be ours. Over 20 years ago, the devil stole a 4-room apartment from us. Well, my new house in Schenectady, NY has 15 rooms in it, and I, my 4 children and 12 of my 17 grandchildren will be able to live together. I am looking forward to God growing a ministry here. Since the day I received your CD with my personal prophetic word, my life has not been the same. You are truly a man after the heart of God. There is money in the mouth of the prophet! Thank you so much for obeying God. I no longer have to walk in the dark!" **(C.F., Schenectady, NY)**

I hear God saying...

The shortage, lack and limitation in your life are over. You are about to experience an explosion of blessings in your life. Do not be surprised when your debts are miraculously and mysteriously cancelled—Just call it FAVOR!

Do not be surprised when unexpected money appears in your life—Just call it FAVOR!

Do not be surprised when loved ones start coming back into your life—Just call it FAVOR!

Do not be surprised when the home that you have always dreamed about manifests right before your eyes. Don't analyze it or second guess it—Just call it FAVOR!

ALL-ENCOMPASSING FAVOR!

*"Thou art worthy, O Lord, to receive glory and
honour and power: for thou hast created all things,
and for thy pleasure they are and were created."*
(Revelation 4:11)

Last year may have had its pitfalls and troubles on every side, but the Holy Spirit is showing me that your current season of financial lack is about to come to an end. The enemy tried to bring some major disturbances in your life so that your eyes would not be opened to the truth of God in you.

Favor Principle #9

**You only go through that of
which you are conscious.**

TESTIMONY #17

"I sowed the $52.00 seed for 52 weeks of uncommon favor. My sister and I have not spoken for almost three years. After I sowed the seed, she called me and we talked for hours. My sister suffered a breakdown, and I prayed that God would restore her mind, and He has answered my prayers. Favor! Thank you, Bishop Jordan and the Company of Prophets for the prophetic word that has elevated my life. Thank you, God, for being the great I Am!"
(Z.C., Chester, VA)

TESTIMONY #18

"I sowed the $52.00 seed for 52 weeks of uncommon favor and God has been blessing me in some uncommon ways! I went to an appointment with a company that I have been dealing with for a few years. Due to a computer error, they owed me money. I received

the first check this past Monday in the amount of $2,220.00. I will receive the rest soon. I also received a letter from my insurance company informing me that they owed me $1,008.00. Praise God!

Due to a strike this past summer, a company that I provide vendor services for was unable to pay me for services rendered. As a result, I was delinquent in paying my car note, and my car was, subsequently, repossessed. The following day after my car was repossessed, I went to a car dealership to try and purchase another car. Due to my credit history, they required me to make a sizeable down-payment for the car. I left and went down the street to another dealership and found the same exact car for sale. They told me that I would need a co-signer for the car. I spoke to my father and he agreed to co-sign for the car. I went back the following day and my father asked me to step out of the office for a second so he could talk to the salesman. Thirty minutes later, my father stepped out of the office with the car keys in his hand, gave them to me and said, "The car is now yours!" My father bought the car for me. I now drive a Mercedes ML500, and I have no car payment! Hallelujah! I have learned to trust God in all things. Thank you, Master Prophet, for your obedience to the voice of God. (**T.T., Torrance, CA**)

Before God allows anything to manifest in your life, God waits for you to give it permission to be. Nothing can be until you consent to its being. Changing your world will require you to change your thinking and produce new concepts of thoughts into being. Until you learn how to enter into the theater of your imagination, you are going to miss the dynamics of God.

Favor Principle #10

**The world is you pressed
out in many forms.**

MANIFOLD FAVOR!

"Seek ye first his kingdom, and his righteousness;
and all these things shall be added unto you."
(Matthew 6:33)

Prosperity cannot be measured by the possession of things, but in the recognition of supply and in the knowledge of free and open access to an inexhaustible storehouse of all that is good or desirable. You must cast away your means of support and create a vacuum in yourself in order for creation to fill it. God can only manifest abundance in your personal economy when you empty yourself of all other visible means of support and lean solely on Him.

Favor Principle #11

You cannot get something for nothing!

TESTIMONY #19

"I sowed the $52.00 seed for 52 weeks of uncommon favor and I received a money miracle! After sowing the seed, I received a check for 800.00 for back child support that was owed to me. Praise God for His faithfulness!" **(S.L. Gretna, LA)**

You have the secret to prosperity within your spirit—your willingness to manifest what you want through your thoughts. Over the next 52 weeks, favor is going to overtake you. Everything that you touch is going to turn to gold. It is impossible to fail. No more seasons of drought. No more seasons of lack. No more seasons of fear. No more seasons of poverty. This time you will experience God's overflow like never before.

TESTIMONY #20

"I sowed the $52.00 seed for 52 weeks of favor and the blessings are still flowing in my life. Today, God showed me incredible favor. $1,800 that was owed to me was released today. Thank you God for uncommon favor!" (**T.S., Houston, TX**)

It is your birthright to be prosperous. God has promised to demonstrate His love for you by showering you with uncommon favor. Did you know that God's favor is priceless and more valuable than money?

TESTIMONY #21

"I sowed the $52.00 seed for 52 weeks of uncommon favor and received an amazing blessing. I am currently in college, and I have to pay my own tuition, with limited assistance. My tuition for the fall semester was $1,300, but I had to pay nothing this fall, and next fall the college is giving me another discount on my spring tuition. I give God the glory, because I did not have the money to pay my tuition, and God came through for me. I walked down the street crying and giving God the glory because He has done great things for me. I do believe the Prophet! God is not finished with me yet. I believe God has broken the spirit of lack off of my back. I am glad to come back and tell others about the glory of God. What God did for me, He will do for others, if only you believe." (**C.M., Perth Amboy, NJ**)

COLOSSAL FAVOR!

"His children will be mighty in the land; the generation
of the upright will be blessed. Wealth and riches are
in his house, and his righteousness endures forever."
(Psalm 112:2-3)

There are two kinds of people in this world: visionaries and provisionaries. The visionary is responsible for casting forth the vision to the people. The provisionary is supernaturally anointed by God to attract finances and resources to support the vision monetarily. They are the money magnets.

YOU ARE A PROVISIONARY!

Being a provisionary has everything to do with the way you think and your willingness to simply obey the voice of God. You were born to create and generate wealth. God wants to put millions in your hand. When you start thinking of yourself as an attractor of money, money will find its way into your life.

Supply is within you and will flow to meet your demands, provided that you fully embrace that you are the supply and that your thoughts produce that which you demand. God gives us all we need to have abundant supply, but He relies on our wisdom to discover the path to that supply.

Favor Principle #12

**You were born to create
and generate wealth.**

TESTIMONY #22

"Master Prophet, I am so excited and encouraged about the prophetic word that I could not wait to share this testimony with

you. I sowed the $52.00 seed for 52 weeks of favor. A few weeks ago, you said that our money would not be late in 2008, that money would start coming to us, and that people who owe us money will start paying what they owe us. Well, it has started already for me and it isn't even 2008 yet!

I am a cashier at Cub Foods. People often leave me tips for bagging their grocery items. Since I sowed the $52.00 seed, many people have been blessing me by saying, "Keep the change." Sometimes it isn't much, but to me, it is called Favor! On December 23, 2007, a customer requested someone to bag his groceries, and I replied, "I'll do it for you, Sir." When I finished bagging his order, he gave me $141.00 and said, "Keep the change." He gave me a $21.70 tip. I began to tell the Lord, thank you, and my mind instantly went back to the things you said about the 52 weeks of uncommon favor. I am going to send another $52.00 seed, because I don't want to miss out on what is going on in the Spirit realm. I love you, Bishop. May God continue to use you!" **(E.P., Minneapolis, MN)**

Now is the time for you to cultivate that which God has placed on the inside of YOU!

Favor Principle #13

Facts are not necessarily the truth!

The facts may say you are bankrupt, but the truth says you are rich. The facts reveal your humanity, but the truth reveals your divinity. You have to understand the difference between truth and facts. The next 52 weeks will be the most exciting weeks of your entire life! Not only will you be able to walk through life knowing that God's favor is upon your life, but you will be able to walk boldly through every test and trial that may come your way, knowing that you cannot fail, you cannot be destroyed and you will not be denied!

This is your year to walk in the consciousness of no lack, because lack no longer has a place in your life. Instead, God wants to ignite the prosperity consciousness within you!

TESTIMONY #23

"The $52.00 seed works in the strangest ways! On December 11, 2007, my business credit rating was 37%. As of December 24, 2007, it is 76%! My new credit rating has repositioned my life, and now I am ready to create that Boaz kind of wealth. Thank you, Master Prophet!" **(G.J., Daleville, AL)**

HUMONGOUS FAVOR!

*"…Believe in the LORD your God, so shall ye be established;
believe his prophets, so shall ye prosper."
(2 Chronicles 20:20)*

God does not want you to take a vow of poverty. He wants you to be prosperous! Prosperity is proof that you are manifesting God's law in your life. The kingdom of God is not a place, but a system in which your mind is at one with the infinite Mind of God. When you live in that state, prosperity will fill your life with riches.

God supplies you with the means to create great riches, prosperity, health and joy in your existence, as long as you remember that He is the source and you live in harmony with His laws. If you do this, no weapon of any kind shall prosper against you. Every trap and snare that the enemy has planned against you shall fail. The Holy Spirit revealed to me that the very things you thought were not possible, God says they are yours, if you believe.

TESTIMONY #24

"I believed the prophet for the 52 weeks of uncommon favor, and decided to make the pledge of $5,200. After pledging the $5,200 seed on Friday, on Monday, I received a phone call from the Mercedes Benz dealer informing me that it was time for my car to be serviced. I informed him that because of my financial situation, I would have to bring the car in later to be serviced. The serviceman told me not to worry about it, to bring the car in to be serviced and I could pay later. That is favor!"
(T.J., Baltimore, MD)

Many people come close to accomplishing their goals. However, the reason they don't accomplish their goals is not just because they don't know how or what to do, sometimes people fail because they don't have proper guidance or sound advice. The more you trust and believe in the prophet, God will open doors that you thought could never be opened. It is time for you to have more, do more, and be more than you ever dreamed possible.

Favor Principle #14

Prosperity is proof that you are manifesting God's law in your life!

TESTIMONY #25

"Since sowing the $52.00 seed, I have seen God's favor manifest in my relationship with my husband. Over the past few weeks, we have been seeing a marriage counselor and we have been able to express our thoughts and emotions within a safe environment. We have been able to release a lot of the hurt, pain, disappointment, betrayal and distrust that we experienced during our marriage. I am now willing to let go of the past and look at the good within him. I can feel healing taking place within our relationship. I truly believe that it was God's uncommon favor that caused my husband to suggest that I join him on Christmas day with his family to allow us to both share the special day with our daughter, and to spend New Year's Eve together. I know that there is still work to be done in the healing process, but the joy, excitement and peace I feel right now is very encouraging. God is bringing healing to my marriage, my husband, my daughter and to me. I thank God for His divine favor." (**C.L., Barbados**)

EXCITABLE FAVOR!

"Whatsoever a man soweth, that shall he also reap."
(Galatians. 6:7)

The seed is giving something to God with the expectation that He will multiply it where you need it the most. Your seed produces a harvest, and your faith brings the actual seed to you. It takes faith for you to sow the seed for the harvest. What is in your hand? What is in your house? What is within your reach? God does not multiply your harvest; He only multiplies your seed.

"Give, and it shall be given unto you; good measure, pressed down, and shaken together, and running over, shall men give into your bosom. For with the same measure that ye mete withal it shall be measured again." (Luke 6:38)

TESTIMONY #26

"The Holy Spirit woke me up early one morning to watch the Power of Prophecy program on television. I requested the free prophecy and every word that you spoke into my life has come to pass. I decided to be obedient to God and sow the $52.00 seed for the 52 weeks of favor. Then I took it a step further and sowed the $300.00 seed to unseat a prophet during the live streaming telecast. What a powerful conversation I had with the prophet when I received the call. Then as a Thanksgiving offering, I sowed a $620.00 seed! The prophetic word was so awesome, I decided to sow the $152.00 seed, and then the $208.00 seed. Why? God led me to do so. It's amazing!

I have never given over $1,000 in less than a month to any ministry, but I know it is God's will, because I received a supernatural answer that money cannot buy. I told my wife about my obedience to God *and explained to her that God raised Bishop Jordan up at such a time as this. Even though she is in Ghana, she knows and understands why the Lord assigned me to sow the money into the Master Prophet's belly instead of wiring it to her. I cherish your letters and e-mails and I am putting them to great use. I know that the Holy Spirit is using me to be a blessing to those around me. I listen to my prophetic word on CD at work, during lunch, and even when I go to sleep at night. Thank you, Master Prophet, for feeding my spirit and sowing so much into my life."* **(J.P., Dover, NJ)**

God has declared the next 52 weeks of favor to be in the realm of substance! God says, because of the favor that has already been placed upon you in this season, you will begin to manifest invisible substance as visible results in your life! Whatever you desire, visualize and put energy towards it and the universe will hand it to you.

Favor Principle #15

Change your feelings and you will change your destiny!

TESTIMONY #27

"I sowed the $52.00 seed for uncommon favor and my favor is starting to unfold. On Christmas Day, I received a telephone call from my brother who has been estranged from the family since my mother's death. The conversation was very good and we were able to talk about things that we have not been able to talk about for a long time. This is uncommon favor! I am fastening my seatbelt for this world-wind of favor that is blowing through my life. I am ready to go wherever it takes me! Thank you, Master Prophet for your obedience to the Spirit." **(S.L., Apopka, FL)**

DIVINE FAVOR!

*"And he said unto his disciples, Therefore, I say unto you, Take
no thought for your life, what ye shall eat; neither for
the body, what ye shall put on. The life is more than
meat, and the body is more than raiment."*
(Luke 12:22-23)

Favor Principle #16

Want attracts want.

All want creates is more want. The Bible declares that the Lord
is your Shepherd; you shall not want. It is time to feast on the
kingdom within. Are you worried about what you are going to
eat or what you are going to wear? If you are, Jesus is reminding
you that you are much more than a meal or a new wardrobe.
God has all of your needs under control.

The raven never considers for one moment where her next meal
will come from. In fact, the raven does not have any money to
buy food, yet knows intuitively that she will eat well each day.
Whenever she gets hungry, food is there, because the raven lives
her life knowing that she is worthy of being taken great care of
by the Master. You are far more valuable than the birds in the
air. Shouldn't you live with the same level of confidence, the
same conviction and knowing that you are worthy of being
taken great care of by God?

TESTIMONY #28

*"I sowed the $52.00 seed, because I wanted the 52 weeks of
uncommon favor to be released in my life. God is giving me back
everything that the devil has stolen from me. My faith in God has*

been restored. I have been taking care of my granddaughter, and now her father is making arrangements for me to start receiving child support payments for her care. I have received numerous gifts, including a new stereo system, a new DVD player and new luggage. I was able to order flowers for my mother and have them delivered to her for Christmas Day! I am really enjoying this unlimited favor that is following me around. I know that God is going to bless me with unlimited money. I feel it and I see it! Thank you for the prophetic word in my life and for the 52 weeks of uncommon favor!" **(R.B., Chicago, IL)**

TESTIMONY #29

"I sowed the $52.00 seed for 52 weeks of favor and my business has exploded. Since sowing the seed, I have acquired more business partners for the New Year, which will allow my business to grow to the next level. I know that 2008 is the year of financial overflow for my business. Thank you, Master Prophet!" **(C.L., Guyana)**

I want you to continue to believe in God's Divine Plan for your life. I want to continue to give you the word of the Lord so that you can discover the realm of possibility; because with God all things are possible, if you only believe.

TESTIMONY #30

"I sowed the $52.00 seed for 52 weeks of favor and God is working in my finances. I received a check in the mail for money owed to me from the sale of my house in 2004. The mortgage company took too much from the sale. My money was released only after sowing the seed, and the check had the number "52" in it! Jesus! I am rolling the loaded dice of FAVOR!" **(Y.B., Teaneck, NJ)**

TESTIMONY #31

"For over 9 months, I had been suffering with a terrible toothache. The pain was so intense that some nights I could not sleep. I did not have dental insurance, so I was unable to undergo the surgery that

was recommended by the dentist. Alternatively, they gave me pain medication to help alleviate the pain, but the pain worsened. I really needed the surgery, but without dental insurance, no one was able to help me. After sowing the $52.00 seed for 52 weeks of favor, a miracle happened. I called one of the dentists on my list and they told me to come into the office immediately. I was amazed because I was so used to hearing the word, "no." I went to the dentist's office and the dentist performed the surgery for no charge! Hallelujah! The pain is gone and I am at peace. Thank you, Master Prophet for allowing me to be a part of the 52 weeks of favor!" **(E.A., Teaneck, NJ)**

BREAKTHROUGH FAVOR!

"God has not given us a spirit of fear, but of power,
and of love, and of a sound mind."
(2 Timothy 1:7)

God is in the process of searching your heart and mind. There are some secrets that you have hidden deep inside your heart. I hear God saying, "The hidden secrets in your heart are your resources for prosperity and real happiness, but they have been locked away." Understanding how to make and achieve goals can bring health, wealth and happiness into the life of any person who is willing to do something about it.

TESTIMONY #32

"After hearing the Master Prophet give the decree to sow a $52.00 seed for 52 weeks of favor, I decided to sow two $52.00 seeds. After sowing the seed, I received an outstanding performance review from my employer, and we received the largest salary increase than we have ever received. The $52.00 dollar seed really does work! I cannot wait to see the remainder of God's favor over the next 52 weeks. Thank you, Master Prophet!" **(B.T., Garland, TX)**

I hear the Holy Spirit saying that you must be bold and firm in this season. The Spirit has also revealed to me that fear has followed you around for a very long time. However, you cannot continue to allow the experiences of your past to plague your future and stop you from moving forward. You have spent most of your life dealing with fear and negativity, but the Holy Spirit is saying, "Put an end to it right now!" Right now, I need you to pause, take a deep breath and repeat after me...

"I am fearfully and wonderfully made.
I am the truth that God says I am."

Fear is a self-fulfilling prophecy, but you choose to let fear become a factor in your life. If you allow fear to overtake your life, then you will reap the results, just as you do when you approach your life with confidence and trust in God.

TESTIMONY #33

"I sowed the $52.00 seed for 52 weeks of favor, and the word of the Lord came to me to pursue a degree in a field that focuses on children. I am now registered to start school online at Kaplan University, pursuing a Bachelor's Degree in Psychology and Child Development. I also experienced God's favor in the application process and did not have to pay the $95.00 application fee. Thank you, Master Prophet, for the prophetic word that has propelled me to higher heights!" **(A.J., Brooklyn, NY)**

Whatever thoughts dominate your mind, those are the thoughts that you will bring into existence. But understand that that thought eventually becomes material. If you are living in poverty or material want, it is probably because you are living in the physical manifestation of your fears!

TESTIMONY #34

"All I can say is the $52.00 seed for uncommon favor does work. My credit report is clearing up and God is giving me favor with the realtor I am working with. We have been living in an extended-stay apartment, and I am believing God that the house I am currently looking at is mine. This could only happen when you have faith and trust in God. Thank you, Master Prophet!" **(T.S., Houston, TX)**

If you are fearful about moving forward in any area of your life, know that something is lying to your eyes and ears and making you believe that you do not have what it takes to be successful. You are in a season where you need some professional and sound advice. You have a lot on your plate right now, and God is saying, do not make another decision until you get your feelings in check. If you are going to walk into the abundance that God has for you in this season, you are going to have to master your emotions.

TESTIMONY #35

"I sowed the $52.00 seed for uncommon favor for myself, my husband and my niece and God is working in our lives already! I received a phone call at the beginning of the week from a production company regarding a secret project that they have been working on for 2 years. They offered me a part on the show! I know this is a result of my obedience to the Master Prophet's cry of 52 weeks of uncommon favor. Thank you, Master Prophet, and thank you, God!" **(B.F. Orange, NJ)**

TESTIMONY #36

"On December 2, 2007, I sowed the $52.00 seed for 52 weeks of favor, and the Master Prophet prophesied that I would experience favor instantly. The very next day, I was asked to work 4 hours overtime, which had not happened in 11 months. Production employees had not been allowed to work any overtime. This was definitely favor and an unexpected blessing! Thank you, God, for your favor!" **(R.D., Slidell, LA)**

TESTIMONY #37

"It works! It works! It works! I am talking about the $52.00 seed for 52 weeks of uncommon favor. Hallelujah! Thank you, Jesus, I have a testimony! After I sowed my $52.00 seed into the church ministry, I received a free trip to Disney World. Thank you, Master Prophet!" **(V.P., Mobile, AL)**

Favor Principle #17

Put an end to fear!

RADICAL FAVOR!

"If any man speak, let him speak as the oracles of God; if any man minister, let him do it as of the ability which God giveth: that God in all things may be glorified through Jesus Christ, to whom be praise and dominion for ever and ever. Amen."
(1 Peter 4:11)

The Holy Spirit revealed to me that gratitude and forgiveness will be your fortune in this season. You are going to have to forget the past and all of the hurt that is attributed to the past. Also, you have to find it in your heart to forgive those who have wronged you in the past. You have proven that you can get upset and become angry with the world. Now, prove that you can walk in oneness and attain all the good that God has for you.

TESTIMONY #38

"I sowed the $52.00 seed for 52 weeks of favor and God is moving in my family in a powerful way. My husband is the only person who is still actively working and bringing in a salary. When he was diagnosed with liver cancer, it was a sharp blow in more ways than one. My home-based business was not financially strong enough to provide for the household. Major decisions had to be made on all levels. We moved forward by the grace of God. My husband was scheduled to begin chemotherapy treatment. In addition, his annual physical required by his company was coming up. We did not mention the cancer, but the examining doctor did not like what she felt during the exam. She immediately requested a battery of tests be done by his primary care physician. We knew there was no way he could camouflage his illness. He would be immediately asked to retire.

A follow-up with the same doctor was scheduled in two weeks time. My husband returned with the reports to his company physician. Despite the findings, the doctor did not recommend that he retire.

She only restricted him to light duty where he could continue to work, with another follow-up scheduled in January, 2008. Praise God for favor!

Also, last week, one of my clients called to place an unexpected Christmas order that has allowed me to take care of some immediate financial concerns; and today I received a check in the mail for money that I did not know I was entitled to until a week ago. The $52.00 seed works! Thank you, Master Prophet." **(M.S., Bronx, NY)**

I hear the Lord saying, You are in a season of change. Everything must change. Nothing can stay the same. This is the season for radical change in the Spirit, to do things drastically different so that your path leads to prosperity.

I can hear the Spirit of the Lord speaking through the clouds of your yesterday saying, "I have deposited great treasures inside of you—treasures that have been hidden; treasures that have not yet been revealed; treasures that will launch you into your destiny. However, to discover these treasures, you must do things differently! Seek My face like never before. For when you truly seek Me and find Me, you will find yourself."

TESTIMONY #39

"After sowing the $52.00 seed for uncommon favor, I made up my mind that I was going to New York for New Year's Eve Service. I had no money, but I had faith in the seed that was sown. I went online and started searching for hotel rooms in New York. The next thing I knew I was booking my hotel stay for 2 nights for the New Year Eve Service.

I decided to go to the mall, because the Master Prophet said I need to bring a brand new wallet to the service. I bought 2 wallets and 2 Coach Bags with a card that had no money on it. That is favor! I am so excited about the opportunity to attend the Service. The $52.00 seed made a way for me to spend New Year's Eve with the Master Prophet. Thank you, Master Prophet, for the opportunity to *see the hand of God move in my life. I will see you on December 31st!"* **(L.H., Raleigh NC)**

Let me warn you, the enemy will fight you tooth and nail, because he doesn't want you to change. The enemy wants you to remain the same, stuck in a perpetual state of confusion and complacency. Even when God spoke to you about moving in the past, fear tackled your emotions and paralyzed you. But when change comes, things change! Let me say that again—when change comes, things change! God will always give us signals that point to change—signals that may not necessarily be obvious or pleasant, but nonetheless, we must recognize the signals and prepare ourselves for change.

TESTIMONY #40

"I sowed the $52.00 seed for 52 weeks of favor, and I received a prophetic word that I will not miss the opportunity for one of my dreams to come true. One of my classmates told me about the dance academy that she worked for; so I decided to research the academy, only to discover that it was Debbie Allen's Dance Academy. I was so excited! I decided to volunteer for the Academy and was able to meet Debbie Allen face-to-face. I've always admired Debbie Allen, and as a child, I wanted to be just like her. I had to keep my composure, but I was jumping inside. I was even able to attend the performance for free. Now that is favor! Thank you, Master Prophet for the prophetic word!" **(T.P., Hawthorne, CA)**

We are living in a world that forces us to adapt to change. When the prophetic word comes into your life, it will always force you to deal with change. Change is NEVER an easy process, yet we face change everyday. God will always put a burning bush in your path to signal that change is on the way—job loss, death, sickness, disease, divorce—but no matter what the signal, unless you yield to the winds of change, you will NEVER reach your God-given, divine destiny.

TESTIMONY #41

"The Master Prophet's decree for the $52.00 seed for 52 weeks of favor has been awesome! Sometimes you have to borrow the seed, and that's exactly what I did to sow my first $52.00 seed for 52 weeks of uncommon favor. After sowing the seed, I received a phone call from a woman who had done an internet search of my uncle, whom we have not seen since August, 2002. She found the name of a relative that still lived in that area for over 50 years. The family member contacted me and gave me the number of the woman who was searching my uncle's name on the internet. After I spoke to the woman, she called me the next day to inform us that she actually met with him and he is doing well. This has been our prayer for years, just to know that he is doing well. It was only after sowing the $52.00 seed for 52 weeks of uncommon favor that this information manifested about my uncle. Thank you Master Prophet. My family is grateful for your ministry." **(C.H., Chicago, IL)**

Favor Principle #18

When change comes, things change.

ESSENTIAL FAVOR!

"Neither height nor depth, nor anything else in all creation,
will be able to separate us from the love of God
that is in Christ Jesus our Lord.
(Romans 8:39)

The enemy is trying to confuse you with thoughts that you do not have what it takes to win. The adversary has one mission and one mission only—to destroy the work of God. The enemy understands that you are God's workman here on earth. So, the only way to thwart the plan of God is by destroying YOU.

But I hear God saying...

"Turn your back on the enemy and see my hand of favor on your life!"

TESTIMONY #42

"I sowed the $52.00 seed for 52 weeks of uncommon favor, and God has been moving in my life ever since. I was in the midst of Christmas shopping, and just 30 miles away from the shopping center, while taking packages from the car into my house, I realized that I did not have the iPod that I had just purchased from the store. I had left it in the shopping cart, in the crowded parking lot of the store. I live about 45 minutes away from the store. The traffic was heavy in the parking lot and the cart attendants were steadily returning the carts back to the store as customers were leaving. I called the store to solicit their help. The customer service representative left her desk and went out to the parking lot to see if she could locate my iPod. Much to her surprise and to mine, the iPod was in the cart. She came back to the phone and said, "You are lucky!" I thought, "No, that's favor!" **(M.P., South Carolina)**

You have allowed the enemy to distract you from your blessings! The spirit of fear, the spirit of doubt and the spirit of worry are the culprits who break our focus. These three demons have a tendency to overwhelm us and cause us to get off track. Did you know that fear is NOT your divine self? Did you know that doubt is NOT the truth of you? Did you know that worry does NOT reflect the meditative thoughts of God in your life? I want to chase those evil spirits out of your life forever!

TESTIMONY #43

"I sowed the $52.00 seed for 52 weeks of favor and I have seen God's hand of protection in my life. I was driving down a dark road, headed to a place I really did not need to go, when I avoided an accident. It could have been an awful encounter, but God's hand of protection was there. I give God the glory, and I am so thankful to be loved by Him. He is constantly showing His favor toward me. I am blessed to be able to think, breathe and function. Thank you, God, for your wondrous works!" **(W.S., Camden, NJ)**

There is no need to go through life confused when the Master Prophet is in the land, a prophet who is ACCURATE, PRECISE and HEARS directly from God. You should not have to struggle every day of your life. You should not have to worry about when you will have your next breakthrough. You should not have to worry about how you are going to pay your next bill.

TESTIMONY #44

"I sowed the $52.00 seed for 52 weeks of uncommon favor and God has been blessing me tremendously! I am having a website designed, which costs $1,000.00. After sowing the seed, I was given the opportunity to pay only $350.00. Praise God for favor! Thank you, God, and thank you, Master Prophet." **(C.M., North Carolina)**

The more you trust and believe in the prophet, God will open doors that you thought could never be opened again. I see things coming into your hands quickly, but first you must believe the prophet and release your faith seed. The word that God has given me for you in this season is going to challenge you to become more proactive in your life and jumpstart that sleeping giant inside of you!

TESTIMONY #45

"I sowed the $52.00 seed for 52 weeks of uncommon favor and God has done an amazing thing in my life. The same week that I sowed the seed, I received a long, overdue settlement from my previous employer, which allowed me to pay all of my bills and buy Christmas gifts for my family. Now, other blessings have been happening in my travel business, and my non-profit organization is projected to be a success in 2008. This is definitely my season for prosperity. Thank you, Master Prophet for the prophetic word that allowed me to keep my faith in God during the rough times. Thank you God, for your Divine Favor!" **(C.M., Vallejo, CA)**

Now, take a deep breath, because I know you thought that all the hell you have been through was because the devil was trying to kill you. For years you have blamed all of your errors and poor decision-making on the enemy. Well, touch yourself and say, "It was all me." Once you come to the revelation that no devil in hell can stop the plan of God for your life, you will open the portals of creativity and allow the waters of prosperity to flow in your life. You are the only one who can abort the plan of God in your life—not your mother, not your father, not your sister, not your brother, not your uncle, not your grandparents. No one or no-thing can stand in the way of what God has for you.

TESTIMONY #46

"In obedience to the Master Prophet, I sowed the $52.00 seed for 52 weeks of favor. A few days after I sowed the seed, I sent my 15-year-old son downstairs to do something for me. For some reason, he was taking longer than usual. I went downstairs to see what was

taking him so long. When I got downstairs, he was talking to a lady, and my son shared with me that he rededicated his life to God! Pray his strength in the Lord! Amen." **(T.S., Houston, TX)**

Did you know that an excuse is just a guarded lie? Say this with me, **"NO MORE EXCUSES!"** No more blaming others for what you are **NOT** doing. No more blaming others for **NOT** walking in the fullness of what God has promised you.

TESTIMONY #47

"Since sowing the $52.00 seed for 52 weeks of favor, I have been extremely blessed with gifts and free rides on the bus! Thank you, Master Prophet!" **(T.W., Baltimore, MD)**

You should not shoulder the weight of your purpose alone. You need the guidance and the wisdom of a seasoned mentor who can shed light on those dark moments in your life, one who can reveal the mind of God in every situation. That is why God has commissioned me to be your personal prophet, so that I can shine the flashlight of life into your darkest moments.

Favor Principle #19

No one or no-thing can stand in the way of what God has for you.

FOCUSED FAVOR!

"For as a man thinketh in his heart, so [is] he..."
(Proverb 23:7)

Many people have the tendency to belittle the treasure that God has placed in them. So many times, we will ignore an idea that seems to just "pop" into our minds; or blow off a money-making suggestion that someone may toss our way; or never put our powerful life story into a book, a story that can change the lives of people all over the world and that has the potential to be a bestseller, all because we do not fully comprehend and value the priceless treasure that God has placed inside of us.

But one decision can change your life forever. One decision to pick up your treasure and assess its value can turn your life around and set you on the road to financial prosperity and success. I hear the Lord saying, "I have placed within you gifts and talents that can change the world and change your quality of life. But you have suppressed my voice and squelched your thirst to bring those gifts and talents into full manifestation."

TESTIMONY #48

"I sowed the $52.00 seed for 52 weeks of favor, and my testimonies keep growing. Doors are opening everyday. A week after I sowed the seed, I was promoted on my job to a higher paying position. The $52.00 seed is powerful and it WORKS!" **(K.C., Newark, NJ)**

Don't sit around limiting yourself! God wants you to **RISE ABOVE!** Rise above your problems! Rise to where there are no pairs of opposites! Rise to your level of greatness! The question is, how bad do you want it? Your level of desire will determine your destiny.

TESTIMONY #49

"I sowed the $52.00 seed for 52 weeks of favor and the favor has already started. The mortgage company financing my home mistakenly withdrew my monthly mortgage from my bank account twice. Right after I sowed the $52.00 seed, they corrected their error and re-deposited the money back into my account. But not only that, the bank also credited my account for $52.00! I never mentioned an amount to the bank; that is the amount they decided to give me. Praise the Lord! That is favor!" **(R.D., Madison, FL)**

The enemy will do whatever it takes to stop you from becoming successful and try to bring a halt to all of your ideas for financial independence. Even during your youthful years, he would whisper harmful things into your ear that would cause you to rebel against your parents and school teachers. The enemy is trying to overthrow your mind and have you think like him. But I hear the Holy Spirit saying, "Enough is enough!"

TESTIMONY #50

"The $52.00 seed just keeps on giving. Praise the Lord! After sowing the seed, I went to the market to purchase some groceries. When I went to the cashier to pay, my total was $42.00. The cashier informed me that I had accumulated $34.00 on my incentive card. I only had to pay $8.00 for my groceries! Then it happened again at another market. I received $23.00 worth of groceries for free because, unknowingly, I had accumulated $23.00 on another incentive card. I can't wait to see what happens next! Thank you, Master Prophet, for your obedience to God's declaration!" **(K.M., London)**

It seems like every time you take two giant steps forward the enemy is there reminding you of your past. He is always trying to maneuver himself into your life and disrupt what you are building. The Holy Spirit wants you to know that you are in a battle for your life and the enemy is not going to play fair.

TESTIMONY #51

"After I sowed the $52.00 seed for 52 weeks of favor, $400.00 showed up in my checking account. I did not question where it came from, because I know it came from sowing the seed of uncommon favor. God has also given me uncommon favor with family members. I decided to sow a second $52.00 seed, because I want the blessings to keep flowing in my life. Thank you, God, the seed is working! And thank you, Master Prophet, for the prophetic word that has changed my life completely!" **(S.M., Waterford, MI)**

The Holy Spirit showed me that you have what it takes to become a millionaire. But there are some things that you have to deal with in order to reach your goal. The word "poverty" must be eliminated from your vocabulary completely. You will not attain wealth or happiness with a poverty mindset. If you want to become a millionaire, you must first be a millionaire in Spirit.

You have been set up by God to break the generational curse of poverty that has been plaguing your family. Think it not strange that lately you have been thinking about financial increase that will eliminate your debt and the debt of your family. You have to grab that desired feeling and walk it out.

TESTIMONY #52

"On December 7, 2007, I sowed the $52.00 seed for 52 weeks of uncommon favor, and by the time I got home, a financial miracle had already visited my home! I opened my mailbox to find a check for $4,074.00, money that has been on hold for several months. Also, my youngest son told me that he wanted to start reading the Master Prophet's book, The Laws of Thinking, with me because he has seen a change in my demeanor since I've been reading the book. Thank you, Master Prophet. Not only that, my daughter has decided to move back home! Hallelujah! Thank you, Master Prophet for your awesome ministry." **(L.L., Newark, NJ)**

The Holy Spirit is challenging you in this season to become more disciplined with your finances and to pay more attention to where you are spending your time. By allowing the right thoughts to penetrate your mind everyday you can begin to expect great things from yourself. The right attitude towards people and money is going to cause the rivers of prosperity to overflow in your life.

God has given you the mental faculties to become as wealthy as you want to be. God wants you to live like the heir of a King. The millionaire in you is waiting for you to turn the lights on and to start manifesting your riches.

- If the bill collectors are hunting you down, YOU NEED THE 52 WEEKS OF FAVOR!
- If your loved ones are hanging out with the wrong crowd, YOU NEED THE 52 WEEKS OF FAVOR!
- If your finances are under attack, YOU NEED THE 52 WEEKS OF FAVOR!

The Holy Spirit is always on time! Even when you think He is late, He is always on time. This statement is true, whether you believe it or not. God is always on time! You are entering into a season where you really need to seek the Father's face in prayer. The Holy Spirit revealed to me that this is not the season for you to give up on your dreams.

The time is now! Get into the water while it is being troubled by the Holy Spirit. No weapon of any kind shall prosper against you in this season. Every thought and deed that the enemy has planned against you shall fail. The very things you thought were not possible, God says, they are yours, if you believe!

> ## Favor Principle #20
>
> **If you want to become a millionaire, you must first be a millionaire in Spirit.**

To sow your $52.00 seed for 52 weeks of uncommon favor and receive your life-changing prophetic word on CD by Master Prophet E. Bernard Jordan, and the Company of Prophets, call 212-316-2177, or you can mail in your seed donation to:

Zoe Ministries
Bishop E. Bernard Jordan
P.O. Box 270
New York, N.Y. 10008
212-316-2177
www.bishopjordan.com

DESTINY IS NOT LEFT UP TO CHANCE, IT IS A MATTER OF CHOICE!